This book was transcribed from one of the thousands of sermons of Bill Vincent. Please realize this as you read this book. Thanks for your purchase and support.

The Secret to Spiritual Strength

Bill Vincent

Published by RWG Publishing, 2021.

While every precaution has been taken in the preparation of this book, the publisher assumes no responsibility for errors or omissions, or for damages resulting from the use of the information contained herein.

THE SECRET TO SPIRITUAL STRENGTH

First edition. November 5, 2021.

Copyright © 2021 Bill Vincent.

Written by Bill Vincent.

Also by Bill Vincent

Building a Prototype Church: Divine Strategies Released
Experience God's Love: By Revival Waves of Glory School of the Supernatural
Glory: Expanding God's Presence
Glory: Increasing God's Presence
Glory: Kingdom Presence of God
Glory: Pursuing God's Presence
Glory: Revival Presence of God
Rapture Revelations: Jesus Is Coming
The Prototype Church: Heaven's Strategies for Today's Church
The Secret Place of God's Power
Transitioning Into a Prototype Church: New Church Arising
Spiritual Warfare Made Simple
Aligning With God's Promises
A Closer Relationship With God
Armed for Battle: Spiritual Warfare Battle Commands
Breakthrough of Spiritual Strongholds
Desperate for God's Presence: Understanding Supernatural Atmospheres
Destroying the Jezebel Spirit: How to Overcome the Spirit Before It Destroys You!
Discerning Your Call of God
Glory: Expanding God's Presence: Discover How to Manifest God's Glory

Glory: Kingdom Presence Of God: Secrets to Becoming Ambassadors of Christ
Satan's Open Doors: Access Denied
Spiritual Warfare: The Complete Collection
The War for Spiritual Battles: Identify Satan's Strategies
Understanding Heaven's Court System: Explosive Life Changing Secrets
A Godly Shaking: Don't Create Waves
Faith: A Connection of God's Power
Global Warning: Prophetic Details Revealed
Overcoming Obstacles
Spiritual Leadership: Kingdom Foundation Principles
Glory: Revival Presence of God: Discover How to Release Revival Glory
Increasing Your Prophetic Gift: Developing a Pure Prophetic Flow
Millions of Churches: Why Is the World Going to Hell?
The Supernatural Realm: Discover Heaven's Secrets
The Unsearchable Riches of Christ: Chosen to be Sons of God
Deep Hunger: God Will Change Your Appetite Toward Him
Defeating the Demonic Realm
Glory: Increasing God's Presence: Discover New Waves of God's Glory
Growing In the Prophetic: Developing a Prophetic Voice
Healing After Divorce: Grace, Mercy and Remarriage
Love is Waiting
Awakening of Miracles: Personal Testimonies of God's Healing Power
Deception and Consequences Revealed: You Shall Know the Truth and the Truth Shall Set You Free
Overcoming the Power of Lust
Are You a Follower of Christ: Discover True Salvation
Cover Up and Save Yourself: Revealing Sexy is Not Sexy
Heaven's Court System: Bringing Justice for All
The Angry Fighter's Story: Harness the Fire Within
The Wrestler: The Pursuit of a Dream

Beginning the Courts of Heaven: Understanding the Basics
Breaking Curses: Legal Rights in the Courts of Heaven
Writing and Publishing a Book: Secrets of a Christian Author
How to Write a Book: Step by Step Guide
The Anointing: Fresh Oil of God's Presence
Spiritual Leadership: Kingdom Foundation Principles Second Edition
The Courts of Heaven: How to Present Your Case
The Jezebel Spirit: Tactics of Jezebel's Control
Heaven's Angels: The Nature and Ranking of Angels
Don't Know What to Do?: Discover Promotion in the Wilderness
Word of the Lord: Prophetic Word for 2020
The Coronavirus Prophecy
Increase Your Anointing: Discover the Supernatural
Apostolic Breakthrough: Birthing God's Purposes
The Healing Power of God: Releasing the Power of the Holy Spirit
The Secret Place of God's Power: Revelations of God's Word
The Rapture: Details of the Second Coming of Christ
Increase of Revelation and Restoration: Reveal, Recover & Restore
Leadership vs Management
Restoration of the Soul: The Presence of God Changes Everything
Building a Prototype Church: The Church is in a Season of Profound of Change
Keys to Receiving Your Miracle: Miracles Happen Today
The Resurrection Power of God: Great Exploits of God
Transitioning to the Prototype Church: The Church is in a Season of Profound of Transition
Waves of Revival: Expect the Unexpected
The Stronghold of Jezebel: A True Story of a Man's Journey
Glory: Pursuing God's Presence: Revealing Secrets
Like a Mighty Rushing Wind
Steps to Revival
Supernatural Power
The Goodness of God

The Secret to Spiritual Strength

Watch for more at https://revivalwavesofgloryministries.com/.

The Secret to Spiritual Strength

The thing God kept speaking to me today was, how many? And how often? might we have robbed ourselves of a blessing? How many times and how often do you think it takes place that you tie down hands or rob yourself of a blessing. Because sometimes we'll react rashly or so negatively about a situation, instead of responding in the way God wants us to respond. And I believe we have blown our blessings. I believe some of this we started talking about last week, but God's saying he wanted me to talk about this part this week, where we need to understand that sometimes it's not the devil. Sometimes it's not, it's not somebody else. But it's we have robbed ourselves of a blessing. You say, oh, God doesn't work that way. You got anybody here ever have a father, everybody has a father, a dad, anybody here has a mother. Everybody has a mother, even no matter what. And I'm telling you when we look at this, let's say for an example, we have two girls, both the same mother, and let's say this one cleans a room. This one gets all the things are taken care of she's supposed to do. And this one does not. There are certain benefits this one's gonna get. Because this one has done and has been obedient to do what they're supposed to do.

The one that was disobedient, and said, I don't want to do it right now. I don't care I don't want to clean my room; it is too messy. They don't receive the blessings, because of obedience, they believe they receive a blessing for their disobedience. And what that means is, they're going to get something because of their obedience. And they're not because of their disobedience. So, the way God looks at us is the same way whenever he tells us to do something, and we don't respond the way we're supposed to. But it actually can rob us. And just so you know, not every time does God necessarily, say, Joshua, you're supposed to write those things down and study them through because I'm just trying to speak to you, doesn't necessarily mean that you have to be obedient by something that God said to you. Sometimes it's about God put laying something on your heart. I went through a season of being robbed by the Spirit, because God told me to give somebody $20 So when I finally caught up, and I realized I shouldn't give them $20, I gave them $40. Because I figured I had some interest to make up. Sometimes we get to the place.

And I believe that sometimes we are moved by our spirit man to do something. But we don't know what we're being moved by. But that is its obedience to responding to the Spirit of God. In Luke Chapter 24, the two disciples who encounter the resurrected Christ were trying to deal with the pain, of numbing disappointment that they were going through. Jesus entered into their world, right, then they're going through an emotional experience. And Jesus shows up. Talking with them, listening to their story, and then exposing their memories of failure and frustration to a new positive light. See, sometimes we don't even realize when we're going through a situation God will turn around, somebody gets involved, turn around, some of you need to understand. Whenever you're going through whatever you're going through. There's a turnaround coming. I don't care where you are. I don't care what you're going through. I don't care how long it's been a turnaround is coming.

Why because God will never allow you to go through more than you can bear. And he showed them how their despondency was caused by a failure to understand God's purpose, and by a lack of faith. See, sometimes we don't even realize Jesus was sent to die and the disciples grieved. If anything, they should have celebrated. he hung on the cross and he died. They wept and they cried, and they mourned. Even when he shows up physically, he had to expose their wounds, expose what was going on, he had to release some things in their midst for them. Finally, they realize, oh, snap, that's Jesus. Jesus resurrected and they had to see it, they had to receive it. And we as a body of Christ, sometimes when you're going through the gloom, when you're going through the Doom, when you're going through the hardship, the lack, all of a sudden you need to realize Jesus is going to come on the scene and he's going to turn around. Then he used the same scripture, Scripture passages, to reinterpret their negative experience and bring new power and hope, through revelation. The most powerful change of all, came when these men experienced the revelation of a risen Jesus. They could not have ever received anything until they receive the revelation. He's not dead. He's not dead. Say our father's remedy for our wounds includes a gift, a service, and a command. To God wants you to be set free. Anybody here has wounds. If you got buttons, you got wounds.

If you got buttons, you got wounds, and that is true. Jesus says I heal the brokenhearted Senator at liberty than that a bruised. See, we must acknowledge that Jesus took our pain, he carried our sorrows. And I'm telling you, he has accomplished at all. And this is God's gift to us. You can't earn healing of your wounds. It's a gift. I don't care about what's going on with some of you people right now. But this is the fact my wife and I know have been healed of much. And because we've been healed and much our lives have changed by much. When you allow the Spirit of God to go in and divide the soul and spirit and deal with the wounds of your heart and set you free a little bit, it will change everything and change who you are itself, something we can't earn, and we must simply receive healing of our wounds. Healing of your wounds is different than deliverance. Many times, when you have a wounded spirit, that's the reason you end up getting bound but that's not the thing that binds you. It is hurt. It's a wound. Somebody wronged you somebody did something, something happened emotionally in your life.

And the next thing, Jesus provided us with the Holy Spirit. And Jesus called him the finger of God. Did you hear that? The Holy Spirit was called by Jesus, the finger of God. One of the Holy Spirit's roles is to reveal the mind of God to us. That's why it's the finger of God sometimes we don't know what's going on and the Holy Spirit will come on the scene and say I'm doing this and all of a sudden things will begin to have peace. Why? Because God put his finger on some things. Say I want you to understand to for God to get us to the point of out of every hidden bitterness, hurt wounds, or rejection. The Finger of God will go on those things to get us to that next place. How many you thought you are fine, and you're set through service, and all of a sudden you feel like oh my goodness, I'm a mess. Because why? Holy Spirit was putting his finger I'm on sometimes you get the whole hand. He didn't just use a finger he got the whole hand. Both of them isn't it right, you're liking what I'm talking about here. Let's go over here See any bitterness God puts his finger on, and hurt God put his finger on any wound, God put his finger on, any rejection God will put his finger on, See God the Holy Spirit knows all things through his inner work. And we are conformed. did you hear this? We are to be conformed to the image of Christ. How do you got to be conformed a whole lot of fingers look how many by for example have done things as you're doing um you know they are wrong?

Has this ever happened to anybody, on this side of the room? Oh, yes, must be back there somewhere. See, that's why you see God said he's conforming us to the image of Christ. But do you know the Holy Spirit is the one who will guide you into all truth? Yet God gets you out of your mess, every time you say I know I'm not supposed to be doing it as you're doing it. The Holy Spirit's trying to guide you out. And you're like La la la la la la la la la la. He said don't do it. Don't do it. No, no, no. I'm on some of these high school people they need Holy Spirit and put his finger on you and say no, no, no. Don't go with those people I used to have a friend who always said, Let's go to the party tonight. And I said for what? He said they're gonna be girls there. I said what else is gonna be there? He said I don't know. Girls are there what more we need so we show up and you know, at that time I was trying to be a good boy. Not for God, for sports. And so, I walked in and they're drinking and they're smoking and they're doing other stuff and I was like, I don't want to be here. He said but girls are here, See I don't care how good a person you are, and I don't care how anointed you are how you think you are you get to put you put yourself in the midst of the den. You are going to get bit you're gonna fall into some stuff

You can't just hang around a bunch of drinking and just think I'm just not going to do it. That was one of those nights as a teenager I went to the bathroom, and I heard police I went out the bathroom window and never looked back but see you don't put yourself in those situations. Well, there are girls there are boys there so come on I'm preaching to high school people tonight we don't go to those kinds of parties. main ingredients at the parties that we go to as cake and ice cream That is what I call a party, popcorn cake ice cream, and movies. Look out PG 13 Maybe if it's okay I'm all we tear it up. Neighbors almost call the police after 10 Because we got the TV too loud Wow. Some of us think it is too funny, see before a cure can be pronounced, we must allow the physician in the form of the Holy Spirit to diagnose the problem. See, God cannot heal you until the problem is diagnosed God cannot heal you until the problem is diagnosed and the Holy Spirit is that finger that will diagnose you. He will say you're doing this how many thoughts at times you were doing something and you're like oh, isn't that bad? You know, I call those pile sins. Little deceit, a little lie, a little fib, a little deceit, little lie, a little fib turns into a liar you say no, I'm not that's a lie.

Say we got to understand I want to say this another time because somebody isn't getting it before a cure can be pronounced, we must allow the great physician in the form of the Holy Spirit to diagnose our problem see the Holy Spirit will diagnose you say see all there it is. it's their daddy asked that PE teacher volleyball coach do you think God put his finger on that let me rephrase that do you think he put a finger on that would you like some pepper with that? All right let's move on. Let Him service your body. Did you hear what I said the Holy Spirit was to service your body he wants to put you up on the rack check your pain change that stuff? Drain out that old, corrupted oil put in fresh oil come on me look at my finger here. See he was a service his body and point out specifics in detail how many have ever taken your car in for an oil change that comes out and they tell you all kinds of stuff like I thought I was getting hold change now you're telling me I need a belt; I need a windshield wiper. I need all this extra stuff. Do you know what that is? That's just like the Holy Spirit. You come in and you get up on the rack and you're up there that he's looking around. He's like Ha-ha, oh yes. Oh, look at that. That's gonna come back and bite her. Hmm. Yes. She almost confessed that one, but she chickened out.

I am hypothetical. Right. But anyway, we're just getting into some stuff tonight. Because God will point out details, he will just put my finger on. That's what he does to us. He doesn't skip us. If anything, I get more fingers in any idea. I get fingers all day long. What are you doing? See Tosh is the only one perfect in the room. holier than now she keeps her wings in the sweatshirt Halloween or summer she has a tough time talking to me in the next one is it's our favorite. This is worse than then cussing for some Christians. It's the word forgiveness. See, sometimes you got to forgive people. See forgiveness is one of the most important ingredients of healing and health to our spirits souls' bad bodies forgiveness while I'm not forgiving her sometimes you got to forgive daily Yeah, I'm stretching my neck nobody getting all this. See sometimes. I want you to hear this God's great remedy for wounded spirits consists of three words this is his top-secret prescription three words are the ingredients for God's remedy of wounded spirits. Number one forgive number two forgive number three forgive you say all that's all three one. Now usually if you got to forgive, you got to do it three times to get it out. Because the first time you're like, I forgive him. Next one, I forgive him. By the last one I forgive him to see, it may be ironic, but you got to understand it's true. The person who suffers the most from unforgiveness is not the unforgiving one. The person who doesn't forgive the faster you release people the faster you get released

Do you believe that I experience the person who forgives receiving a greater blessing than the one who gets forgiven, did you hear what I said? When you forgive you get a bigger blessing than the person you're forgiven it's like you could just say I forgive you, Cha-Ching, some of you like in my sermon, sometimes you got to forgive them you don't make the devil mad when they're in your face giving you a hard time just look at them and say I forgive you, it is hilarious I get they'll get turned hot real quick surely when I forgive you come on people see God command you to forgive says garbage man I forgive you next time pick up my trash but I forgive you. See forgiveness involves recognizing that God has forgiven us even though we don't deserve it. See, it's easy to forgive somebody when you have realized you didn't deserve to get forgiven. So of course, the people you forgive don't always deserve it, but you just do it I forgive them can't come like this I forgive and release them to God wow you can't kick on and to the field see we must also release the person from the debt we feel he or she owes. In other words, when you forgive somebody you cannot expect that they're gonna forgive you back. that'd be like you're saying I just want to let you know I apologize and release you and forgive you. And then you wait for saying all right. Don't you have anything to say? No in the things of God you release them. But you don't need to expect anything in return. That's why forgiving is its I forgive them and release them. I've never preached this part before I forgive you and I release you, isn't that good, and I forgive them and release them. We must accept, we must accept the person who offended us for who they are. See, that's what's fairly forgiving is I forgive you, just the way you are.

See a lot of us like to put conditions on forgiveness. I forgive you when you forgive me, and then I'll forgive you also when you change. That's not the way it works. You forgive them, and you release them of anything and everything. And then you also forgive them so much. Just the way they are. Thank you, Lord. This means that you're releasing the other person from the responsibility of having to meet our needs in any way. Here's the true definition in Vincent's dictionary, Vince's dictionary,

I've only got one definition. This is my first one putting in there. We must forgive. This is forgiveness. We must forgive forget and get on with it. Did you hear that we must forgive forget and get on with it? How many have ever held for unforgiveness and dragged you down for days weeks of forgiveness? Every time you see somebody reminds you of them or you see the person, you're like grr, forgive, forget, and get on with it. Do you want to do that? So, does anybody want to do that? We've always said that saying if you're still talking about it, you're not over it. You're supposed to get on with it. Get rid of it. Say if you've forgiven and you've forgotten, then you can move on.

See some specialized situations require more specific ministry. These involve people being affected by the power of inheritance of spiritual family conditions such as chronic alcoholism, sexual perversions, child molestation, and other types of social and emotional abuse. I'm telling you, no matter what you're going through and what you are forgiven, some of these chronic problems cause you to have to forgive much more. How many know somebody has been molested you They got to be forgiven much. You got to forgive that dirty dirtbag much. Man, I didn't call him that for you. I call him that for me. And you got to understand such negative spiritual influences must be renounced. See if you have gone through that kind of trauma. You don't just forgive, but you also renounce, why? Because you're breaking the curse. All the forgiveness in the world is not going to change the chronic spiritual situation in your life. If you have any of those things I just really build. It's only when you renounce them after you have forgiven them that will break the very assignment. Other situations are like ungodly soul ties. Some of you in this room have ungodly soul ties. Soul ties with a certain friend can be ungodly. You can have a friend but it can't be ungodly soul ties, that ungodly soul tie has to be severed, and if you truly want a friend that you have an ungodly soul tie with and you're going through the things of God and going to church and all those things you better break the soul tie otherwise God's gonna have to break the relationship to help you survive.

Hope you understand stand this why because it's emotional dependency when you have an unhealthy soul tight and emotional dependency you'll have for the other some people are dependent on their mommy and it's okay when a mommy wants I mean there is a level of okay and that but at the same time there's also a dependence that comes can be unhealthy that's why I've always thought it was wrong for a teenage boy to be sleeping with his mommy or a teenage girl sleeping with their mom it doesn't matter, come on its one thing to do it an hour to hang out while you're watching a movie or something and you're just all just hanging out mode but I'm telling you when it comes to bedtime it can be a weird thing and I'm not talking about one night or something because somebody was sick I'm talking about every night it becomes an unhealthy soul tie.

See these co-dependencies must also be renounced and broken in the name of Jesus, by far the most prevalent cause of broken hearts and spiritual wounds are rejection, did you hear what I said? The number one cause for broken hearts and wounds is the rejection I didn't get a teddy bear I didn't get a fluffy bear. Did you get a fluffy bear, it would be hilarious if he did not have been like yeah almost buy one just for spite hallelujah, see sometimes we don't even realize how many people have had had a spirit of rejection upon them might even happen in the womb rejected before they were even born or rejected by their dad or rejected by their mom or rejected by people at school, come on the family will reject you. Sometimes that spirit will hang on inside of your heart, and you don't even realize how much it is there and it becomes the very root of the wound in your life. I had a spirit of rejection come up all my life at age 11, my favorite aunt of all time, I mean an aunt that I just I adored I love just as well as my mother. I love your kids. We just all played and had an enjoyable time shooting BB guns at each other. Don't do that. I all kinds of stuff. I mean, we just were always serious stuff. But I'm telling you, I'd done it one thousand times ride my bike to their house and just hang out all day, done. One thousand times did it every day. Because she had a problem with my mom during this one specific time, I rode my bike there. She without saying one word to me, took my bike, put it in the trunk. So, we're going somewhere helped me get in the car. And when she got, she pulled up to my house, got out of the car, took my bike and threw it out, and told me to get out of the car. Just because she had a problem with my mom. And that rejection came in my life like a ton of bricks at 11 years old and this innocent boy who had never known any nasty, demonic things that day opened up into a spirit of wounds and hurts and pain that turned to anger and rage and self-destruction.

You say how do you know all this it had to be revealed through the deliverance sometimes you don't even realize how bad something is. But our history many times will cause you to have many years lost because of a spirit of rejection some people feel like they're being rejected before they even get started. Some people don't want to try new friends because you're afraid of rejection is not to keep your same little group as you don't want to mess with anybody new because you don't want to face rejection. Even though you didn't know if you were gonna hit a teddy bear, you still had no friend to give you a teddy bear, but that still could be a spirit of rejection couldn't oh not that one heart. See, rejection is a sense of being involved, or are or unlocked, unloved, or unwanted by those whom we want or need love from. The Litchfield school is full of unloved and unwanted children. Peer rejection is running rapidly. And some of the most popular people are the most projected ones. There is only the way they are in school because at home they have no love. They have no kindness. They have no respect no nothing. They're nothing but hated at home and mistreated and abused in every situation. And at school. They have to raise themselves above everybody else because that's the only place they got, be a lot harder to hate some of the people if you can see them in the Spirit. See it's a sense of being unloved or unwanted. And I'm telling you to reject rejection is a feeling of being excluded. Like being picked last of a softball game or kickball. Thank you, Lord. See, I moved a lot, and man after that spirit of rejection came up all my life. It didn't matter when you move, they don't know how good you are. They don't know so they don't pick you for anything. And so, every time I move there, I was the last person standing in the dugout they go yes, we'll take him whatever. So, I had to prove myself. Sometimes the spirit of rejection is because you have been rejected you always have to prove yourself to everyone. See, it's like being on the outside always looking in.

In the US it has been recorded. One out of five people has been rejected. So, this group here, one of you may be living in the spirit of rejection. This group right here, one of you could be living in a spirit of rejection on average. On average you go into some houses and in some neighborhoods, you got the whole bunch or none. See people suffering from rejection often come from a single-parent family. Did you know that especially when you got multiple siblings? One is always going to act like they're not loved as much as the other. Well, when she was sick, she got to watch TV. And I was homesick, and I have a stay in bed. Let's come in from a spirit of rejection. Or like I like to call it bla bla bla bla bla. See many marriages are dysfunctional. See some people have spouses a mom and a dad in the same home. But that doesn't mean a hill of beans when one is not relating to the other, sometimes marriage is better to separate, and I know God is not in favor of divorce, but some marriages are just staying together for the children having affairs and cheating and doing all kinds of stuff and mistreated children because of it. And I'm telling you, I don't know about you, but it'd be better for somebody to go home, got a lot of that in Litchfield school district a whole lot of parents not together See, these children often admit to suffering from chronic loneliness, depression and advanced stages of rebellion and bad fruit and self-destructive behavior. See, whenever we are young and we're going through this kind of self-destructive behavior, we'll say things like I hate you to our mom. Why because it's coming from a negative wound. I wish I were dead; how many know that is not nice I hate myself Let's come from a deep wound. See an alarming number of these people. Either has thought seriously have committed suicide or have attempted to commit suicide, patience, kindness, great love is needed for children of a broken home kindness, patience love is needed what God just said to me, you're gonna love this. And one of the ways that God says love is shown is spelled R U L E S, it took you the E to figure it out. Sometimes it takes rules. Rules will be the difference between how much love they are receiving sometimes. How many know children need rules. Even big ones. They need structure. stay in school. Don't be a mule stay in school. So, you got to understand, in the midst of this, sometimes rules are the way God will even cause us to understand his love.

See, the opposite of rejection is acceptance. See, if you feel accepted. It breaks the spirit of rejection. You want to know when you know there's been a spirit of rejection working. You go to a friend's house for a couple of days. You're gonna feel accepted the whole time she's gone. You go to a friend's house. You feel more accepted when she's gone. You know, why is that spirit of rejections tries to come upon you. And it's using each other as a comparison. You say I don't believe that. Then why is it every time I'm preaching to you to Don't look at me funny? Why is that every time you start to go through something or get in the midst of something, you say what about her? And why is it when you're getting put on the spot about something and you get told to do something? You'll be like, well, she didn't, okay, you don't have to answer anything. Just move on. Good stuff. See regardless of how rejection begins, it could come through illegitimate birth, poverty, parental rejection handling problems, unfair comparisons, and others, or self-rejection sometimes nobody else is rejecting you reject yourself. How many have ever looked in the mirror and had rejection I don't like my nose I don't like my ears I don't like this I got a pimple on my forehead, there is more where that came from, you can carry a spirit of rejection you know what usually happens is something you don't like about yourself you're going to find a man or a woman in your life that's going to like something you don't like about yourself and your appearance. You'll be like I just don't like this I don't like that and you're going to have somebody that's gonna think it's adorable see you don't be like I don't know about this and somebody's gonna be like oh look at that unfortunately for every negative emotion and rejection or reaction and attitude there can be a corresponding demonic spirit, did you hear this? With every attitude that can have a demonic spirit with it everyone some of you I know I know your children are the best ones in the world. I mean I just know nobody there has an attitude ever. Sometimes that attitude can be nothing but demonic they just turn it on sometimes all you have to be is asked to do something

Oh, my goodness. Me today you ask youth to take out to the garbage man they just almost get mad I don't know about you. But whenever I was a kid, you had a bunch of chores, and you didn't get paid I'm on you take out the garbage you did the dishes you cleaned your room you had to do all causes yard work. And when you had all done it was always something new to do. You never put your hand out to say where it is, would like a dance? preach it, brother I've known kids to spend more time making a sign about chores than they did the chores, hypothetical, that is good stuff I don't have to read all my notes on this we'll see most people tend to react to rejection internally where no one else can see it you're gonna be in the middle of a crowded room receive a spirit of rejection because the way somebody responds to you and not even let on that anything happened, a friend, for example, could sit with you every lunch break every day sit with you talk to you have fun with you every day. One day they don't even look at you don't even say a word to you and walk by you and go sit with somebody else. That spirit of rejection can come upon you it can you say oh no it would never you'd be like could at least tell me and it's good stuff. How many of you don't realize how many things are gonna leave tonight? Whichever the case remedies are the same. We must submit all the patterns of darkness to God and his light brings light to all the darkness, internal reaction to rejection includes increased loneliness. Self-Pity, depression, moodiness, outright despair, despondency, and a sense of hopelessness.

Nobody ever had this you know sometimes people will say I'm just quiet come on but that's not always the case sometimes it's the spirit rejection that's caused the quietness. These strongholds eventually result in death wishes see when you carry a spirit of rejection long enough you want to die, you just want to just hand them a knife and say good luck, just fall off the roof and let gravity help you , is that wrong, it's wrong but see that spirit of rejection really is not that smart thoughts are particularly dangerous because they often are hidden from the eyes of friends and family, see when we carry a spirit of rejection we try not to let anybody know it, we try to make rage our friend I'm not rejected I'm just bad see, in every one of these situations the way of the cross is the only way to be home, no one suffer more rejection the Jesus Christ yeah he gave all mankind me all mankind for the spirit of rejection or mistreatment he has already given all to overcome that spirit of rejection, see Jesus didn't die from his wounds or brutality on his during the crucifixion he died from a broken heart, you say I don't believe that, right before he died he wept right before he died he began to cry out Lord forgive them for they know not what they do. Sorry, that's not funny as a private thing and I'm telling you that was coming from a broken place let's close with this everyone in this room you got to me know this almost sounds derogatory but it's true. You got to turn on the Holy Spirit You got to turn on the Holy Spirit you say what does that mean? Like flipping on a light switch. You got to turn on you got to just turn on the Holy Spirit. Just got to turn it on. Turn him on.

In other words, bring the fingers put your finger on it you know allow God to put his finger on seeing I love it whenever God because we're like Come Holy Spirit come right now and then here he comes with his fingers and we try to cover up the see here God can see it anyway and we got to let the Lord specifically point out better now hurts, wounds rejections that may be hidden in your life. Don't try to conjure it up. Let him bring those things to your remembrance. Some of you the simplest prayer can be, Lord. When did the spirit of rejection come in, pray that prayer, and wait? Many times, you'll remember, and then when you remember, you can break it all. You can ask for forgiveness, and you can renounce any part of it and be free. The next one is that favorite one, forgive especially forgive the person or persons who caused you to receive hurt or pain. See, remember forgiveness is an act of your will. And forgiveness is not just starting talking to him again. You can't just start talking to him again. Well, that's the same as forgiveness. No. That's like just talking to somebody instead of saying I'm sorry. When you hurt her, you should say I'm sorry? And you should forgive her, you should forgive her. And when you hurt her, you got to understand no matter what you're going through, we've got to release one another. The third one is to repent from your anger and bitterness. Take responsibility for what you do. And stop giving fingers to somebody else. Somebody thought it was the other fingers. Get your minds out of the gutter. I give that finger, you need help. See, if you allow God to put his finger on you, you'll start pointing to others you know why? Because you're going to give up or tap out, see our salvation or the delivers from rejection are found and the love of Jesus Christ. The Lord forgives you. He does he forgives you. Even when you don't deserve it. He forgives you. Even when he's going to have to do it again very soon, he forgives you. Even when you barely talked to him you do a lot of thinking on God, but he said a lot your mouth isn't moving.

I wonder where you got that, he forgives you. Even when you don't deserve it, we got to embrace Papa. Embrace the father's love. Let him fill you with a father encounter is your you hear me? You need a father encounter. You need God to encounter you. As a father. You need a god to encounter you as a big daddy. Allow him to cause the Holy Spirit to get his fingers going. Fingers doing the walking, some of you going to have a whole hand to God upon you. That means every finger is on a place every one of them Some of you would like to have a Valentine present, the biggest bear biggest teddy bear you could ever want. His name is Jesus. You can cuddle with Jesus you can love on Jesus. You can wrap your arms around Jesus. Don't be frightened. Oh, you aren't going marring him someday, get rid of that homophobe thing going on. I got a gown waiting on me. It's gonna be after I die but that's all right. Or after I go to heaven. Some people are trying them on now. Are you ready for that? are you ready? You receive this, do you receive this. So, I'm going to ask you to all pray this prayer because you need to receive it to good prayer. There are no tricks up my sleeves with this one. We just go pray a prayer. Say, Lord Jesus, I thank you for your son, for your Father, for the Father, for the Holy Spirit. And I ask for the finger of God the Holy Spirit to put his finger on anything and everything in my life to deliver me in Jesus' name.

And I for those who want to be hardcore, say Lord Jesus do whatever you have to do hmm, I didn't hear it. Say do whatever I have to do. You have to do whatever you have to do. I'll move your mouth for you. Do it now. Oh, it works. If you want to be delivered you mama Sita if you want to be set free and be happy and Jubilee, say Lord do whatever you have to do to do it now, Lord Jesus do whatever you have to do it now, do it now yes would be bad we could have so many hairs How about you go first? You almost seem like you prayed it anyway might as well do it I said do it oh sorry. Praise God, this is good stuff. You should take this home and draft an essay on it before you get any more TV, if she doesn't get any, neither do you Oh you're right for One that'd be fun. And one right what he got out of this tonight; I forgive my mom for not letting me drive as much as I want to know why she doesn't let you drive as much as you want to. She had to move the seat every time you get the car other than I hate worse.

I love when they brought the new Cadillacs out. I'm done preaching if you didn't realize it, they brought the new Cadillacs out and they had a seat memory button. So, you could let people use your car, do whatever, and then when you got in it, you just pushed a button that was memory and went back to where you had it to begin with. I'm on lockdown. lock me up, thank you, Lord, as some of this tonight was required for driver's license, you say why permit driving? Two? You say why? Because if you're angry and you're behind the wheel of a car, that doesn't mix, they don't mix, note worse than a mad driver to get a car, come on you forget what you're driving you to know that kitten I've seen you we when you're upset That's good stuff. Thank goodness be healed already. You stop it. Be healed right now, Jesus. Receive it tonight. Most of you receive it tonight. I don't know if we did a city for this, but I have something to say. Okay. Ryan, God told me to tell you tonight. Your mom loves you. Her actions don't show it sometimes. But God told me to tell you tonight that she loves you very much. There are some things in her and some things in you that collide. And gal says I'm going to prove to you how much she does love you in the days ahead. But it's gonna get worse before it gets better. She does love you. Sometimes she doesn't like you at all. But she does. God says she does. Hallelujah, hallelujah, though we just have praise. Thank you, Lord. Hallelujah

All right here God wants to give homework tonight God told me this is homework, and everybody needs to do it. And the baby doesn't count. You can't use the baby on this but every person in this place needs to say this to somebody and tell him why. Paul is not home. So, Sam's already messed up. I can't give some love to Ryan. Anyway. But you're supposed to say this. I love you because and give a reason to somebody in your house. No can't be a pet or baby you're gonna have a baby but it's gonna be extra because everybody's going to be like I love you, Arianna. Some of this is supposed to deliver you a little bit, you say all this can't be what we're supposed to do. Yes, you're you need to do it. We all deserve what God said. Why? Because some of us aren't loving and respecting one another enough. So, God said He wants us to say I love you. And God already told me I can't tell my wife. So, I only have that one or that one. Yes, that's you're both a runner-up such for sure. You can do more than one, you don't have to limit it. But God said to do it to one why? Because you need to find the love you got to get your feelings out um All right, it's in there you go look at Sam. I said Dude I'm on some of you need to break off your homophobic personalities and all that. Lord, we just give you praise right now we cleanse this place of it that is not a view we seal what you are saying in Jesus' name we just give you praise and glory for what you're doing hallelujah we will see you tomorrow night if you need to CDC Tabitha or McKenna actually

Don't miss out!

Visit the website below and you can sign up to receive emails whenever Bill Vincent publishes a new book. There's no charge and no obligation.

https://books2read.com/r/B-A-XHBC-VOETB

BOOKS 2 READ

Connecting independent readers to independent writers.

Also by Bill Vincent

Building a Prototype Church: Divine Strategies Released
Experience God's Love: By Revival Waves of Glory School of the Supernatural
Glory: Expanding God's Presence
Glory: Increasing God's Presence
Glory: Kingdom Presence of God
Glory: Pursuing God's Presence
Glory: Revival Presence of God
Rapture Revelations: Jesus Is Coming
The Prototype Church: Heaven's Strategies for Today's Church
The Secret Place of God's Power
Transitioning Into a Prototype Church: New Church Arising
Spiritual Warfare Made Simple
Aligning With God's Promises
A Closer Relationship With God
Armed for Battle: Spiritual Warfare Battle Commands
Breakthrough of Spiritual Strongholds
Desperate for God's Presence: Understanding Supernatural Atmospheres
Destroying the Jezebel Spirit: How to Overcome the Spirit Before It Destroys You!
Discerning Your Call of God
Glory: Expanding God's Presence: Discover How to Manifest God's Glory

Glory: Kingdom Presence Of God: Secrets to Becoming Ambassadors of Christ
Satan's Open Doors: Access Denied
Spiritual Warfare: The Complete Collection
The War for Spiritual Battles: Identify Satan's Strategies
Understanding Heaven's Court System: Explosive Life Changing Secrets
A Godly Shaking: Don't Create Waves
Faith: A Connection of God's Power
Global Warning: Prophetic Details Revealed
Overcoming Obstacles
Spiritual Leadership: Kingdom Foundation Principles
Glory: Revival Presence of God: Discover How to Release Revival Glory
Increasing Your Prophetic Gift: Developing a Pure Prophetic Flow
Millions of Churches: Why Is the World Going to Hell?
The Supernatural Realm: Discover Heaven's Secrets
The Unsearchable Riches of Christ: Chosen to be Sons of God
Deep Hunger: God Will Change Your Appetite Toward Him
Defeating the Demonic Realm
Glory: Increasing God's Presence: Discover New Waves of God's Glory
Growing In the Prophetic: Developing a Prophetic Voice
Healing After Divorce: Grace, Mercy and Remarriage
Love is Waiting
Awakening of Miracles: Personal Testimonies of God's Healing Power
Deception and Consequences Revealed: You Shall Know the Truth and the Truth Shall Set You Free
Overcoming the Power of Lust
Are You a Follower of Christ: Discover True Salvation
Cover Up and Save Yourself: Revealing Sexy is Not Sexy
Heaven's Court System: Bringing Justice for All
The Angry Fighter's Story: Harness the Fire Within
The Wrestler: The Pursuit of a Dream

Beginning the Courts of Heaven: Understanding the Basics
Breaking Curses: Legal Rights in the Courts of Heaven
Writing and Publishing a Book: Secrets of a Christian Author
How to Write a Book: Step by Step Guide
The Anointing: Fresh Oil of God's Presence
Spiritual Leadership: Kingdom Foundation Principles Second Edition
The Courts of Heaven: How to Present Your Case
The Jezebel Spirit: Tactics of Jezebel's Control
Heaven's Angels: The Nature and Ranking of Angels
Don't Know What to Do?: Discover Promotion in the Wilderness
Word of the Lord: Prophetic Word for 2020
The Coronavirus Prophecy
Increase Your Anointing: Discover the Supernatural
Apostolic Breakthrough: Birthing God's Purposes
The Healing Power of God: Releasing the Power of the Holy Spirit
The Secret Place of God's Power: Revelations of God's Word
The Rapture: Details of the Second Coming of Christ
Increase of Revelation and Restoration: Reveal, Recover & Restore
Leadership vs Management
Restoration of the Soul: The Presence of God Changes Everything
Building a Prototype Church: The Church is in a Season of Profound of Change
Keys to Receiving Your Miracle: Miracles Happen Today
The Resurrection Power of God: Great Exploits of God
Transitioning to the Prototype Church: The Church is in a Season of Profound of Transition
Waves of Revival: Expect the Unexpected
The Stronghold of Jezebel: A True Story of a Man's Journey
Glory: Pursuing God's Presence: Revealing Secrets
Like a Mighty Rushing Wind
Steps to Revival
Supernatural Power
The Goodness of God

The Secret to Spiritual Strength

Watch for more at https://revivalwavesofgloryministries.com/.

About the Author

Bill Vincent is no stranger to understanding the power of God. Not only has he spent over twenty years as a Minister with a strong prophetic anointing, he is now also an Apostle and Author with Revival Waves of Glory Ministries in Litchfield, IL. Along with his wife, Tabitha, he, leads a team providing apostolic oversight in all aspects of ministry, including service, personal ministry and Godly character.

Bill offers a wide range of writings and teachings from deliverance, to experiencing presence of God and developing Apostolic cutting edge Church structure. Drawing on the power of the Holy Spirit through years of experience in Revival, Spiritual Sensitivity, and deliverance ministry, Bill now focuses mainly on pursuing the Presence of God and breaking the power of the devil off of people's lives.

His books 50 and counting has since helped many people to overcome the spirits and curses of Satan. For more information or to keep up with Bill's latest releases, please visit www.revivalwavesofgloryministries.com. To contact Bill, feel free to follow him on twitter @revivalwaves.

Read more at https://revivalwavesofgloryministries.com/.

About the Publisher

Accepting manuscripts in the most categories. We love to help people get their words available to the world.

Revival Waves of Glory focus is to provide more options to be published. We do traditional paperbacks, hardcovers, audio books and ebooks all over the world. A traditional royalty-based publisher that offers self-publishing options, Revival Waves provides a very author friendly and transparent publishing process, with President Bill Vincent involved in the full process of your book. Send us your manuscript and we will contact you as soon as possible.

Contact: Bill Vincent at rwgpublishing@yahoo.com www.rwgpublishing.com

www.ingramcontent.com/pod-product-compliance
Lightning Source LLC
LaVergne TN
LVHW042005060526
838200LV00041B/1881